Say it Silently

Alison Brett and Tina Michelle

Spiraling Compass Publishing

Paperback ISBN: 978-1-958238-03-5

E-book ISBN: 978-1-958238-05-9

First print edition: 2023

Spiraling Compass Publishing LLC

Prior Lake, MN

www.spiralingcompasspublishing.com

Contents

To family. To friends. To those we love and who love us,

despite our mistakes and imperfections.

Relationships

Her Heart is Colder than her Hand

She's here, but she's not

She's warm, but she's cold

She's mine, but in secret

She's nice, but she's mean

She's decent, but obscene

She's mine, but in secret

She's loving, but hurtful

She's near, but she's distant

She's here, but she's drifting

Yes, shadows fall where lovers land.

Her heart is colder than her hand.

The Man in Me

They tell me to dress up and act like a girl

But I have resolved to be me

The man who's inside me, he screams to come out

The man they're refusing to see.

Discretely, the sun peeks his head through the clouds

I swear I've got nothing to hide

But what they are seeing when I fake a smile

Is not what I'm feeling inside.

I want to fit in, but I always feel lost

I'm constantly misunderstood

When I am exposing the man that I am

They claim I am up to no good.

I have no control over how I'm portrayed

Their ignorance flows like the sea

But one thing is certain, I will not concede

They won't change the man who's in me.

Black Skies

You caused me hurt

I feel the pain

There is no turning back.

I'm hearing talk

About blue skies

But all I see is black.

The demons dance

Inside my head

They mock each move I make.

I cannot breathe

I see your face

With every breath I take.

I try to sleep

But it's no use

The demons never do.

So, I just sit here

Wide awake

And pass them off to you.

Don't try to run

Don't try to hide

There's nowhere else to go.

For when my black skies

Turn to blue

You'll be the first to know.

Horribly Familiar

Heartache and fallacies are on repeat as my darkest realities return.

Somewhat intrigued and on the edge of my seat, I stay, though I know it's a curse.

You're drawing me in just like he did, but we all know that history gets repeated.

When will I stop this? When will I learn? Not today. Yet again, I'm defeated.

When will I have enough love for myself. Not today. I am feeling depleted.

What must I have done to deserve this? Every kiss is filled with toxicity.

And why would I leave knowing well that I'd be on to the next one, never finding felicity?

Love You Backwards

Always yelling, always fighting,

Always filled with rage.

Always saying never,

Never turning past the page.

Always hurting, always crying,

Always calling names.

Never feeling good enough,

And always playing games.

Never saying sorry,

Never feeling loved.

But it's so clear, the love is there,

I can't say that enough.

I know it's real. It's how I feel,

I know it often staggers.

Just know if I can't love you right,

I'll always love you backwards.

Feeling Claustrophobic

The walls are closing in on me

I'm having trouble breathing

I've felt like this since yesterday,

The day you said you're leaving.

I need more space, I need some air

I just need to forget you

You want to tear my world apart

But I'm not going to let you.

What kind of powers do you hold

To cause my life to shatter?

You only care about yourself

I've realized I don't matter.

I promise you I won't succumb

These walls won't hold me longer

You think that you have made me weak

You've only made me stronger.

I'm feeling claustrophobic now

And you're the reason for it

I will not let you drag me down

I'm going to ignore it.

Evanescence

Your memory is evanescent

Fading, and fleeting, and passing

Yielding, withdrawing, departing

Until one day, it's barely a thought.

Some days, I really do miss it

Yearning, and aching, and wanting

Searching for something that's missing

Until it's unreachably gone.

Something's amiss in between us

Twisting, and breaking, and bending

Repelling each other like magnets

Fractured apart without cause.

Your memory is evanescent

Slipping, and fleeing, and drifting

Yielding, withdrawing departing

And now, it's unreachably gone.

Treasure Box

I have a box of treasures

They're under lock and key

I keep them safely hidden

Treasures only I can see.

The box is filled with secrets

And puzzles never solved

My troubles rest inside there

Waiting to become resolved.

I opened it on Tuesday

But couldn't yet decide

Which problems I should tackle

And which ones to set aside.

I saw your photo in there

And turned it upside down

I cannot face the pain yet

Of not having you around.

I closed my box of treasures

And lay there for awhile

The shining stars above me

Seemed to emulate your smile.

My box is now reopened

I let the light shine through

I hold your photo to my heart,

And smile back at you.

Love Paranoia

Every time you touch my skin it echoes through my body.

Every word you say to me echoes through my mind.

I pray to the lord for just one chance to stop and press rewind.

But time is so evasive, and it starts to slip away.

Every time you're far from me, it echoes in the silence.

Every time I'm far from you, it echoes in my thoughts.

I ponder with repetition about all the shoulds and oughts.

But time is so evasive, and it starts to slip away.

Every time I wake, my dreams echo like a song.

Every time I sleep, the echoes disappear.

I try to sleep more often, but I long to feel you near.

So, I toss and turn and echo as more time slips away.

Every time I, every time I, every time I echo...

But it starts to, it starts to, you start to slip away.

Every time I, every time I, every time I echo...

Stop, stop, stop, and press rewind.

Dreams echo, dreams echo, dreams echo like a song.

I toss and turn and echo and try to turn them off.

The Day You Died, I Felt Nothing

The day you died, I felt nothing...

And everything.

I felt sorrow through the smiles.

I felt excitement through the pain.

I felt heartbreak through the love...

And poison in my veins.

I felt teardrops, concern, confusion, and loss.

I felt resentment and relief, but something felt so off.

The day you died, I felt nothing

But it rocked me to my core.

You're alive as ever, but dead to me, I'm sure.

Blissfully Bizarre Dreams

I often dream I'm falling

But it's you who hits the ground

And then I wake up sleeping

And you're nowhere to be found.

I'm walking on the ceiling

And beneath me, there's no floor

I'm craving your attention,

But don't want you anymore.

I'm dancing on an island

Wearing nothing but my hat

I laugh when I imagine

Just what you would think of that!

You're wanting to control me

But there are no shackles here

My slumber brings me freedom

And diminishes my fear.

And now that I've awoken

And you still invade my home,

I'm going back to dreaming,

Where I'm blissfully alone.

Plagued by Nightmares

It broke me watching you kiss her

And watching you turn to drugs.

I fell apart when you left me,

And as if that weren't enough...

You were unaffected,

As if our love were useless.

To you, maybe it was.

It's clear you're dark and ruthless.

It feels unreal to me.

My eyes must be deceiving me.

Then again, it's crystal clear

You're done and won't be needing me.

I can't believe you'd do this.

The pain, it cuts so deep,

Until I open up my eyes

And see you're still asleep.

Away From You

Gone for just a second

In my mind, it feels like years

Try to just ignore it

I am swallowed by my fears.

Quick breaths are followed by shaking

In my chest, I am physically aching

No matter how much I try to distract

My heart feels your absence. My body reacts.

A knot in my stomach slipped down from my throat

Makes me feel like my insides are bound to explode

Endless threats in the world loom to end your existence

Helpless at home, I try hard to resist this.

So, forcefields of love escape from my body

But they don't quite reach you. Instead, they just harm me

I beg of you, don't go, even just for a moment

Because a moment feels like years

And for years, I am broken.

Just for the Night

Colder winds have whispered, but tonight feels like the end

Being with you is all I can imagine.

Now that it is over, I want to just pretend

I want to make believe it didn't happen.

I feel you in the shadows. I see you in my dreams

It is hard to come to terms that you're not here.

I toss and turn and reach for you every single night

I can't accept the fact that you're not near.

Come back, my love, just for tonight. If you leave again, I swear I won't complain.

For I'm willing now to lose you twice and feel the pain once more

If it means that I can be with you again.

Giving You Up

Giving you up wasn't easy

But I realized you were a drug

Drawing me in and keeping me there

Never letting enough be enough.

I realize I can't stop the bleeding

From this hole that you pierced through my veins

I'm sure I'll resent you forever

And won't know a day without rain.

Giving you up was like giving me up

Our bodies and souls intertwined

Unraveling us was unraveling me

But if you ask, I will tell you I'm fine.

Giving you up wasn't easy

It was hard, but I'd do it again

You once were my lover, but soon I'll recover

I'll mourn you, but only 'til then.

Wicked Fantasies

I have some wicked fantasies of bringing harm to others

It's just like stories with a twist, in books without their covers.

But these are people who I love. Why would I have these visions?

That's why I won't indulge myself in making rash decisions.

I wish I could control my mind and free myself from malice

The truth is I'm a caring soul, but others find me callous.

There must be something wrong with me, but how do I resolve it?

A puzzle with a missing piece, I don't know how to solve it.

Perhaps, I should just get away and hide out undercover

So I don't act upon my thoughts of bringing harm to others.

ALISON BRETT AND TINA MICHELLE

Overdue Therapy

He snuck in my bedroom when I was just ten

He swore to me he'd never do it again.

When I was eleven and mom was asleep

He did it again and said, "Don't make a peep."

At thirteen, he entered, and I tried to scream

He covered my mouth and said, "It's just a dream."

At fifteen, he tried, and I blackened his eye

He threatened if I gave him up, I would die.

Afraid to tell mom, I just hopped on a train

And knew I would never be back there again.

Alone by myself, I had no cash to spend

So, suddenly sex had become my best friend.

I slept with some strangers from all parts of town

I see, all this time, you've been writing this down.

Will I be okay; Is there hope to reclaim?

Can I live a normal life and clear my name?

I need some advice, but your face reveals sorrow

I'll pay you today, and I'll come back tomorrow.

Domestic Abuse

You are the King

You slapped me again; I'm not angry with you
I know it's because I behave like I do.

I can't get it right, and your dinner was cold
I haven't yet learned to just do as I'm told.

If I make you smile, may I sleep in our bed?
The couch is too hard, and it's hurting my head.

A pillow would help, and a blanket or two
I promise I'll try to accommodate you.

For you are the king, and I am your pawn
Just sit here, relax, and I'll go mow the lawn.

And right after that, I'll wash all your clothes
I'll go to our garden and pick you a rose.

When my chores are done, I'm taking a seat

At the foot of your chair, to massage both your feet.

Don't hurt me again; I'll do as you say

I'm hoping you won't ever send me away.

Hierarchy

Where are you in my hierarchy?

What can you do for me?

Just shower me with all your time,

'Cause my time isn't free.

You say that you're not satisfied.

You think I really care?

Another person would be glad

To see me standing there.

You dial my number every day

Want me to talk to you.

Has it escaped your foolish mind

I've better things to do?

You can't admit that you are wrong

And I am always right.

I'm certain when you steal my time,

You do it out of spite.

Where are you in my hierarchy?

I guess we'll have to see.

One thing's for sure, no matter what,

You'll never be like me!

You Can't Hurt Me Anymore

The rain it pours, the wind it blows

You can't hurt me anymore.

The anger in your face still shows

You can't hurt me anymore.

You try to find the words to say

You can't hurt me anymore.

For I have sent you far away

You can't hurt me anymore.

You want to let yourself back in

You can't hurt me anymore.

Admit defeat, you'll never win

You can't hurt me anymore.

And now it is your turn to cry

You can't hurt me anymore.

I've finally learned to say goodbye

You can't hurt me anymore.

What I have been through, no one knows

You can't hurt me anymore.

My door is locked, forever closed

You can't hurt me anymore.

Crazy Love

Closure

Come back to me, my love. It wasn't really over

And now the time has finally come to seek a bit of closure.

Years have passed between us. The memories have faded

But all this time, you've lingered here, and all this time, I've waited.

Waited just to say goodbye and share our final words

So come, my dear. Sit here awhile, even though it hurts.

The wine we'll sip for hours will help us to forgive

All the pain and heartache that the years have left us with.

And in the final hours, we'll practice letting go

The real thing happened quickly. It's time to do it slow.

So drive away, but this time don't forget to wave goodbye

Let's give ourselves the closure we've been needing all this time.

The Tower

Take me back to the tower again

The tower of hopes and dreams

The tower of inspiration

The tower of Kings and Queens.

Take me back to the tower again

Before we are set aflame

Before we are haunted by memories

And drenched in moats of pain.

Take me back to the tower again

It isn't yet too late

But we're approaching the final hour

Left vulnerable at the gate.

Take me back to the tower again

If not, I will go it alone

But a tower is only a tower

And it's nothing on my own.

Krazy Karma

You say I'm crazy. Am I, though?

You're judging someone you don't know.

Perhaps it's you who isn't right.

How do you even sleep at night?

Words of contempt you know so well.

Beware, or I may cast a spell!

Oh, are you scared? As you should be.

Karma is crazier than me!

Stoop to Your Level

Sometimes, I want to stoop to your level

Pretend you mean nothing to me

Leave your latest message on read

Ignore you for weeks after leaving your bed

Tell all our friends that you don't mean a thing

Go find the one who will be the next fling

Pretend you're a placeholder and nothing more

When you ask where it's going, tell you I'm just not sure

Tell you I want to but don't know the remedy

While lying in bed, intertwining extremities

Sometimes, I just want to stoop to your level

But I'll tell you why I never do

I think it's a shame that you push me away,

And I like that I'm nothing like you.

Retribution

Standing at the alter

Dressed in black and white

Waiting for my love to cross the aisle.

Getting kind of antsy

So are friends and family

I guess we have been waiting for awhile.

"Dude, she isn't coming,"

My Best Man softly whispers

My eyes tear up when I realize he is right.

So, I walk back down the aisle

Hurt

Betrayed

Ashamed

And I go back home, alone, without a wife.

Now, it's three years later

And I walk these London streets

I moved here with a new girl on my arm.

Walking down the alley,

I nearly collide with someone

I then realize it is her. She's with her mum.

I ask her how she's been,

Still not knowing why she left me

She says she's doing well but still alone.

I tell her it should have been us

I tell her it still could be

She shakes her head and simply tells me, "No."

The new girl runs off angry

I don't really care though

Three years, I've always missed what used to be.

"Well, I really should be going."

Her words cut like a knife

I plead for her to stay and be with me.

She says she has to go now

She says never to call her

I ask her if she'll change her resolution.

She says she learned I cheated

Two weeks before the wedding

And leaving me at the alter was retribution.

Mother's Embrace

So many thoughts that run through my head

A baby, a child, dependent on me

I am still just a child myself

I thought I was careful; how can this be?

I'm like a bird, still learning to fly

Not ready to take the next step on my own

My mom was able to handle it though

She took care of me before she was grown.

Just like a ghost that no one can see

This poor child's dad is nowhere to be found

I will need help looking after my child

He needs to be cared for when I'm not around.

Needing to study and make it through school

I'm thinking this is an impossible feat

I wouldn't dream about giving him up

But I must provide for him so he can eat.

I'm guessing I'll have to figure things out

Perhaps, everything will just fall into place

Others have told me that nothing compares

To the warmth of a child in a mother's embrace.

Unconditional Love

The first time you went to jail, I didn't know how to react.

I yelled at you profusely, and then longed to take it back.

Though I was filled with rage, and couldn't understand it,

I knew within my heart, you shouldn't be abandoned.

I came to bail you out, even though I thought I couldn't.

I even chose to forgive you, even though I thought I wouldn't.

I know sometimes when you mess up, I do seem kind of heartless.

Just know, no matter what you do, I'll still love you regardless.

Trying to Get Home

Walking down the crowded streets

I'm trying to get home

Several days and several weeks

I'm trying to get home.

No familiarity

I'm trying to get home

Obstacles in front of me

I'm trying to get home.

Every street sign looks the same

I'm trying to get home

No one here who knows my name

I'm trying to get home.

I don't know where you can be

I'm trying to get home

Home is only you and me

Without you, there's no home.

Still, I wander on and on

I'm trying to get home

I refuse to see you're gone

There is no place like home.

Solitude

Dependency

Dependency consumes me
How do I say goodbye?
I'd say I have control now
But I do not choose to lie.

We had a conversation
Just moments before now
I'm dialing your number
Letting go, I don't know how.

The wind outside is laughing
The moon, he shakes his head
They know I wish to prosper
But stay lying here instead.

Inside, I'll light a fire
And with one final blow
Dependency, you'll crumble
And at last, I'll let you go.

The moon, he will be smiling

The wind will set me free

And I will hold my head high

Walking independently.

Solitude Standing

Solitude is here again

She's knocking on my door

"Go away. I've seen you here

too many times before."

I cannot shed another tear

My eyes are way too dry

Still wishing you were with me now

Not understanding why.

I'd scream, but I've forgotten how

Would anybody care?

Do you, by chance, see what I feel

And feel my empty stare?

I'm looking for a life that's real

Can't hide behind my lies

Okay, come in, dear Solitude

I've never liked goodbyes.

Empty Room

Empty room

Empty walls

Solitude settling

Feeling small.

Reaching out

No one there

Empty room

Feeling bare.

Vision blurry

Voices stir

Empty mirror

Don't know her.

Knocking sound

Upon the door

Feeling nothing

Wanting more.

Empty room?

I see a chair

But I am sitting

On the floor.

I Walk the Ocean on My Own

Walking along the ocean

The breeze goes through my hair

A million problems left behind

While here, I just don't care.

The waves are so hypnotic

They put me in a trance

Deep down, I feel like dying

But now I want to dance!

Lovers holding hands

Kissing and Caressing

But me, I walk alone

And yet consider it a blessing.

Alone with my thoughts

Alone with my dreams

Maybe not alone forever

But for now, that's how it seems.

I often like imagining

I've made a home in there

Rolling with the ocean waves

Beyond a single care.

I walk the ocean on my own

My favorite place to be

Perhaps, someday, I'll find the one

To walk along with me.

Whispers in the Rain

Darkness in the shadows

Teardrops from the sky

Lullabies of nature on repeat.

A couple hoots from owls

A couple croaks from frogs

Crickets in the grass and at my feet.

Feeling kind of lonely

Though many here surround me

It's just becoming clear, I'm not like them.

I listen to their songs

Move forward to their rhythm

And yet, I still just feel I need a friend.

Darkness in the shadows

Pleasure next to pain

Hoping to find comfort

From whispers in the rain.

Every Morning

Every morning when I wake up, I have my cup of tea.

Wild berry with a splash of honey.

Every morning, after tea, I go pick up miss Rose,

My exuberant and bashful little bunny.

I read a chapter and a half.

Then, I move my bookmark to that page.

I listen to comedy and have a laugh.

Then, I put miss Rose back in her cage.

Almost without fail, this brings me to ten o'clock.

I turn the TV on for just an hour, and then I turn it off.

I have some avocado toast and pour myself some water.

Then, I look through some old pictures, of me and my two daughters.

I give them a call around 1, their time. They're usually pretty busy,

But they talk to me for half an hour and tell me that they miss me.

By three o'clock, I'm fairly bored and often take a nap.

Usually, when I wake up, I set miss Rose back on my lap.

I rock in my chair in the living room until the sun goes down.

At times, it's pretty lonely here with no one else around.

I always watch the sunsets. It's the prettiest thing I've seen.

Then I rest my head and go to bed, before repeating my routine.

Loss

Eighty-seven

Eighty-seven isn't just a number
It hasn't been to me in quite some time.

Eighty-seven holds a lot of meaning
Eighty-seven's always on my mind.

Eighty-seven days have gone by slowly
Since the day my grandpa lost his life.

Eighty-seven was his favorite number
It also was his age the day he died.

Now eighty-seven's sewn into my jersey
So I can have him near me when I play.

Eighty-seven's always in a hurry
But eighty-seven's always here to stay.

Years from now when I no longer wear it

And even when I am no longer here

Eighty-seven will live on forever

And someone will hold eighty-seven dear.

Appointed as an Angel

I had this horrible dream that I was going to crash.

I didn't even get to say goodbye.

I wish I had just one more breath to hold you in the light,

But I didn't get to wake before I died.

Darling, please don't worry. I am now an Angel.

The lord just told me it's my time to go.

There's work for me in Heaven. There are people here who need me.

Some of them are people who you know.

Some of them are pets. The puppies are my favorite.

Just like me, they left the world too young.

But way up here, we're cherished. We're loved and we're protected,

And way down there, you sing the songs we've sung.

Know that I'm alive. It's your heart that keeps me living.

Without you, I'd be nothing more on Earth.

And though my body left you, know that I'm still here.

Death was just the start of my rebirth.

In loving memory of Matt and Alyssa

Your Funeral

When I was at your funeral

I wasn't really there

My soul, it left my body,

Affected by despair.

The flowers were all turning black

Their wilted leaves were gray

I heard a gentle whisper

Same voice I hear today.

Your shadow, lurking in the grass

And no one else could see

The ghost I see so clearly

Who lives inside of me.

I know you hear me when I call

And when I say your name

Your funeral has changed me

I'll never be the same.

When I was at your funeral

Your body buried deep

A part of me went with you

Eternally, I sleep.

My life is at a standstill now

It has been for so long

Until I'm called to heaven,

I need to carry on.

Daisy

A world that's filled with flowers

A world that's filled with rain

One moment, feeling happiness

The next, enduring pain.

My tears that fall like raindrops

Resemble morning dew

A quiet tinge of hopelessness

I'm intertwined with you.

Envisioning a rainbow

I see her disappear

She'd surely show her face again

If only you were here.

A sky that is eternal

A hole that runs so deep

A flower such as Daisy lies

Forever sound asleep.

I dream of endless pastures

A place I'll someday be

Where Daisy will awaken

And the rainbow sets me free.

In loving memory of Daisy

Depression

Bleeding in the Water

My lips fell off and I fell silent, staring at the moon.

Dripping with insanity inside the blue lagoon.

Blackened be the late-night sky on porcelain, my skin.

Reddened be my bleeding heart, that's drowning deep within.

Purposeful Solitude

It's 2:00am, and I'm in my car, alone, in an empty lot.

It's 2:00am, and I know I should go home, but I do not.

Another hour quickly passes by.

Unbeknownst to me, I've stopped looking at the time.

Sad melodies on the radio consume me.

They threaten to unravel and undo me.

I imagine myself turning into nothingness.

I imagine myself happy to be done with this.

But happiness can only just be fantasized.

Because the idea of pain is becoming so romanticized.

Finding enlightenment in the darkest of our days.

We sometimes almost seem to like the pain.

Sitting with it a while longer just to see.

Hoping to feel something stronger when we breathe.

Toying with the notion that reality

is made up of a million little fallacies.

We think we know the answers, but we don't.

We think we will get past this, but we won't.

It's 4:00am, and I am sitting in my car.

I am sad, but I find peace amongst the stars.

Moments in the Gaps

Depression and sadness go hand in hand, but there are times when they aren't linked.

There are times when happiness does prevail, and sadness starts to sink.

But even when sadness hides its face, depression latches tight.

Happiness for a moment.

Depression for all the nights.

Moments of bliss can push depression to the hollow depths of the mind.

But the second those moments pass, depression returns each time.

So consistent, so dependable, and so loyal to its host.

You can count on depression to be there.

Lurking and silent, an unwanted ghost.

Depression and sadness go hand in hand, but sometimes that statement is wrong.

So, please... remember:

A smile on my face doesn't mean depression is gone.

Time Keeps Ticking

I'm not watching the clock.

It is watching me.

No.

It is taunting me.

With every tick of the hour hand,

I get older.

Slower.

But time stays steady.

Steadily moving and taking away.

Taking me with it.

Memories fade.

Can't slow it down and take time to think.

Pen to a pad, I am losing my ink.

I Hide it Well

Plans on Saturday night? Sure, I guess, why not.

Drinks at the bar to follow that? Let's do it. Bring it on.

Why do I look tired? I guess I don't really know.

Really, I'm feeling down, but I'd never let that show.

Why'd I bail on the concert, three days before the event?

It's just been a hectic week. I'm feeling kind of spent.

What did I do instead? Not much. I just lay low.

Really, I'm feeling down, but I don't want them to know.

I don't want them to question, to wonder, or to worry.

So, when it gets to be too much, I leave them in a hurry.

I'm hurting on the inside, but they will never know it.

Really, I am feeling down, but never will I show it.

I'm Not Here

Sitting at the table, on a Wednesday afternoon.

The kids are going on about their day.

Though I try to listen, I don't hear a single word.

They wonder why I don't have much to say.

I don't have much to say cause I'm not present.

I'm here but I'm not here at the same time.

I'm trying hard to be more than a body in the room.

But I guess I'm just not in that frame of mind.

Call me a bad person. Call me a bad parent.

You can call me anything you'd like.

There's nothing you can call me that I haven't called myself.

I'm already aware it isn't right.

This isn't a decision. This isn't a quick fix.

It isn't that I'm being inattentive.

This is a disease. A warping of the mind.

I'm here, but uncontrollably I'm pensive.

Sitting at the table, on a Wednesday afternoon.

Eye contact and smiling ear to ear.

My kids are so excited with every single word.

Please don't let them know that I'm not here.

Heaven

I often sit and wonder

Just how nice Heaven would be

I contemplate that death

May be a better life for me.

A world where there's no hatred

And a world where there's no pain

A place where I can smile

And I can be myself again.

Just what would Heaven look like?

Greener trees, a bluer sky?

A gift of angel wings

Which would enable me to fly?

The clouds would be my neighbors

And the sun and moon, my friends

I'd see the loves I've lost

And walk a path that never ends.

What is there for me down here?

Would they even know I'm gone?

Wherever I may live,

It would be nice to just belong.

But what if I'm in Heaven,

And it's not what I've foreseen?

Can I just turn around

And go back to my old routine?

I guess I'll hang around here

For a little while more

And Heaven, he shall wait

Until I knock upon his door.

Two Weeks to Live

The doctors told me yesterday, I have two weeks to live

So, I will be receiving now; I've nothing left to give.

Please take me on a journey to a place I've never been

A castle high, where I can hear a harp and violin.

I want a bed of roses, where the petals never die

And answers to my questions without ever asking why.

And while we're on last wishes, build a house up in a tree

And throw a treehouse party, have some caviar and tea.

But do you think that I should leave myself one day to cry?

I'm fairly young and quite unsure that I'm prepared to die.

Shadows of the Night

They're multiplying day by day, the shadows of the night

The last one took my hand and said, "Come closer to the light."

I said, "You take me for a fool," and pulled my hand away

I know someday I'll have to die, but that won't be today.

The other shadows danced around to let their presence shine

I would have stayed to watch the dance if they were friends of mine.

So, like a shadow of the night, I slipped away, myself

I will not be forgotten like the bookends on a shelf.

I headed to a place where I can feel alive and free

But much to my complete dismay, the shadows followed me.

I guess until I finally take that step into the light

I will be overshadowed by the shadows of the night.

My Heart's Forever Numb

I get great satisfaction when other people cry

I often laugh at funerals when friends and family die.

There is a sense of comfort to know I'm not alone

To see someone depressed like me, it makes me feel at home.

Some people say I'm crazy; they say that I'm insane

They simply fail to understand; they do not feel my pain.

So many have been sheltered; their eyes are always closed

I never had that luxury; my mind has been exposed.

Don't try to seek compassion; I'm empty as a drum

My heart is somewhere deep inside, but it's forever numb.

I'm Allergic

I'm allergic to sunshine; I'm allergic to light.

I only feel peace when the day turns to night.

I'm allergic to people; I'm allergic to crowds.

I flourish in silence, don't like when it's loud.

I'm allergic to kisses; I'm allergic to love.

My solitude fits like a hand in a glove.

I'm allergic to counseling; I'm allergic to care.

When I'm seeking guidance, there's nobody there.

I'm allergic to writing; Nonetheless, I still do.

My personal channel, my way to get through.

Endlessly Seeking

I've been searching for something all my life,

And still, I haven't found it.

I'm sure that I am close, but I don't care.

I've wasted too much time to just keep circling around it.

I've paid the price for wanting something rare.

I know when I grow older, and someday want for nothing,

This failure will still be my one regret.

I'll long to turn the clock back, to stop and press rewind,

But we all know that life can't be reset.

I'm standing at a crossroads.

I'm forced to make a choice.

Keep searching, or move on and keep on wanting.

It doesn't really matter which way I choose to go,

Because either way the road ahead is daunting.

I Hate the Holidays

I always find myself depressed around this time of year

While others walk around and say they're spreading Christmas cheer.

I think about my loved ones lost, no longer here with me

It's them I want, and not the presents underneath the tree.

I feel my anger escalate when caroling goes on

With all the evil in this world, they're breaking out in song!

I don't want any part of it, although you think it's great

I will be like a bear; I'll skip these months and hibernate.

So, you go shopping, sing your carols, spread undying cheer

I will be standing in the shadows, waiting for next year.

Hidden Feelings

I'm going to get through this

Said the voices in my head

Emotions in a whirlwind

Through the clouds above my bed.

I'm going to escape me,

Leave my inner soul behind

Lost in my darkest secrets

That are trapped within my mind.

I dare not to release them

To evade the scrutiny

Of those who are judgmental,

Casting shadows over me.

Forever, I am silenced

Feelings locked within a cage

Great loneliness and heartache,

Sorrow, emptiness, and rage.

I'm going to get through this

Said the voices in my head

Advising me my thoughts are

Often better left unsaid.

Anger

A Stupid Poem

I tried to write a poem today, but nothing came to mind.

I tried to tell a story, but I stopped and pressed rewind.

Nothing made sense.

It was hard to find the words.

So, I threw away the pen and pad and yelled and cried and cursed.

I'm overreacting you say?

Maybe, but then again, no.

All I wanted to do today was write a stupid poem.

Violence

Lilies and Daffodils, something pretty,

To set me free from this violent city.

Safe in my mind from this vast gaping hell.

I was an Angel, but somehow, I fell.

The Earth keeps spinning with monsters within.

They haunt me and hunt me. They know where I've been.

I'm always checking what's over my shoulder.

Waiting for someone to tell me it's over.

Wishing Well

Wishing well, I wish you well

But here I am, grown up

I can't believe I was a fool

Believing in this stuff

I thought I wished for simple things

But not one wish came true

No love. No friendship. What's the use?

There's nothing left to do

Farewell to my wishing well

I wish you'd just dry out

I don't need you or any wish

To know what life's about.

I Hate this Whole World

I hate this whole world and everyone in it

And who was the genius who thought to begin it?

There's no peace on Earth, just hatred and violence

The rain won't stop talking, the sun lives in silence.

There is no escape from a world so corrupted

A world lacking kindness, where lives are disrupted.

I hate this whole world; there's no doubt about it

Been silent too long now. I'm ready to shout it...

I HATE THIS WHOLE WORLD!

Regrets

Watching the leaves fall

As the Angry Tree

Tosses each one to the ground

Heart racing fast

I hear no sound

But the wind

That has surrounded me

Drawing me closer and closer

To this angry tree.

"Stop!" I yell.

"Just stop!" My face is wet.

I look down. The leaves are dry.

I look up. It isn't mist or rain.

It's regret.

So I cry...

But the leaves keep falling

And the wind won't let me be.

"I hate you Angry Tree! I hate you!

I'm not talking to you...

I'm talking to me."

It's Not Puzzling

It's my puzzle

Can't you see

This is what

makes sense to me!

The pieces fit

When I am here

All alone

With no one near.

No missing piece

No missing link

My brain has space

And time to think.

Don't stand so close

As if you care

YOUR puzzle's waiting

Over there!

When Lies Were the Truth

They're liars, they're traitors. I see through them all.

They promise to catch me but laugh when I fall.

No one can be trusted. I won't turn my back,

To set myself up for a schemeful attack.

The raindrops keep falling, no clouds in the sky.

The forecasted weather is even a lie.

My secrets uncovered, not sure who I told.

But they surged like wildfire, festered like mold.

My girlfriend, she canceled; She said she was ill,

The same night my friend saw her dancing with Bill.

And I was adopted but told otherwise.

My parents were just spewing lies upon lies.

I often wish I could go back to my youth,

When I didn't know better and lies were the truth.

Life Behind Bars

I've been behind bars now for nearly ten years

It feels like it's been twenty-five

And after my trauma experienced here,

I'm lucky that I'm still alive.

They say I killed three, but I think it was one

I do recall killing my wife

Like nails on a chalkboard, she drove me insane

I'm probably in here for life.

I'm trapped in this hell hole with no place to go

I guess there's not much I can do

The trash that surrounds me, I don't have the words

Like color that's missing its hue.

If I could escape here and kill all the guards,

I'd do it without a delay

But since that's not likely, I'll sit myself down

Before it is me who's the prey.

Homelessness and Addiction

No Place to Go

I never imagined that I'd end up here
Not having a place to call home
I'm hearing the birds sing and watching the deer
My outfit is all that I own.

The ground is so cold and I don't have a coat
I'm famished and don't have a dime
The end is a story I already wrote
It's only a matter of time.

If anyone out there would kindly assist
You'd help me much more than you know
But sadly, I know that I wouldn't be missed
If I should decide to let go.

I'll sleep here some more now and pray for the best

I hope someone answers my prayers

A soft bed where I would be able to rest,

Provided by someone who cares.

Blackjack

My funds are gone, I lost it all

My wife, my car, my home

My kids won't even speak with me

And now, I'm all alone.

I'm on my way, to try again

An eagle in the night

And maybe now my luck will change

I'll play my cards just right.

The vulture has the cards laid out

His claws are sinking in

I'll swoop down and refuse to fold

I'm going for the win.

I won this round, my chips are in

The eagle bets it all

And since I am already down,

There's nowhere left to fall.

I lost it now; there's nothing left

I'll have to call a friend

And ask if I can borrow funds

So I can try again.

30 Days Sober

Drinks have been in me since 1985,

Working their magic and bringing new life.

But damn, when she left me, I knew it was time

To put down the bottle and leave it behind.

Now, thirty days sober has been the goal for a while.

It's just 30 days, I can say with a smile.

But one day goes by, and I don't even think.

I pick up a bottle and happily drink.

As each swig goes down, that happiness fades.

Failure and loneliness take happiness' place.

It is time for a change. Truly it is.

I won't get her back, but I'll be there for my kids.

Thirty days sober remains to be seen,

But today I have made it. I am seven days clean.

Water and Wine

No matter how much I get, it never feels enough.

So come on and please pour me one more glass.

I know you've said before that next time I'm cut off.

But just one more, and that is all I ask.

Please don't tell the others.

They wouldn't understand it.

They just don't fully understand my need.

But you do understand it.

It's why you still oblige.

It's you who never saw me as a fiend.

I know it's getting old. I know there is a cutoff.

If this is it and truly the last time,

Please just be a friend to me and give me something small.

Give me water but convince me that it's wine.

Pain Self Inflicted

I'm sitting in this padded room where all I see is white

They said I slit my wrists and nearly took my life last night.

I don't recall a single thing; the night was just a blur

My mom would worry if she knew; please keep this all from her.

It's starting to come back to me; I swallowed something green

And someone had convinced me I was in a time machine.

I traveled back, in space and time, to 1993

And seeing you again, I guess, just got the best of me.

But when the drugs had all worn off, I hit an all-time low

And realized, in reality, I had no place to go.

I took a few more pills, and I was at a masquerade

I think that shortly after that was when I grabbed the blade.

I'm sitting here and pondering how long they'll make me stay

At least I know I won't be self-inflicting pain today.

Miracle Drug

Blurred, but no more black and white

Surrounded by colors so vivid

Not sure what these blue pills are

Don't take them away, I'd be livid.

People cry, I hear them sing

The sun and the moon have collided

Every person has joined hands

The world is no longer divided.

Children dancing everywhere

There isn't a cloud in the sky now

I will be here for awhile

Not planning on saying goodbye now.

Just another pill or two

I'm flying above all the fire

I am feeling so alive

There's no way to climb any higher.

Now, I'm in this room again

The walls have become white and narrow

Compress placed upon my head

The wings fallen off of the sparrow.

I have hit the lowest ground

My pills are no longer around me

Someone get me out of here

And put me back where you had found me.

My whole life depends on it

This miracle drug keeps me going

If I die because I live

Sometimes it's just better not knowing.

Delusions and Dissociations

Disturbed

Above my head, upon the ceiling, a spider spins its web.

I feel as if I'm caught in it, but I am lying in my bed.

Just watching. Just feeling. Just breathing. Just sinking.

I'm drowning. I'm hurting. I'm healing. I'm thinking.

There are voices downstairs that are speaking quite gently.

I can't hear the words, but I listen intently.

They are traveling closer, sending chills down my spine.

I'm worried. I'm fearful. I'm crazy. I'm fine.

Voices get closer and they're speaking against me.

They're angry. They're mad. They're cruel. They detest me.

They tell me to do things I don't want to do.

They tell me to hate me, hate them, and hate you.

I'm drowning. I'm hurting. I'm fearful. I'm worried.

The spider above me runs off in a hurry.

My Husband will Wake Me

I'm really confused and my mind always races

When people come visit, I don't recognize faces.

They say that they know me and they are related

They say I am weary, and I'm always sedated.

Don't know why my husband does not come to see me

They told me he's gone, but I know that cannot be.

We spoke on the phone, that was just this past Sunday

Or was that my son? Maybe it was on Monday.

I must find my car keys, I'm late for my meeting

They put me in charge of the coffee and seating.

The nurse has arrived now, and I'm feeling drowsy

That needle again, always makes me feel lousy.

My eyes are so heavy, submissive to slumber

My husband will wake me; he has my room number.

Tea Party

Molly Gail and Hannah Lee,

Won't you join me for some tea?

Wendy Ann and Laura Sue,

Would you like to join us too?

Becca Rae and Sally Fern,

You stay there. It's not your turn.

Okay, ladies, let's sit down

Grab your teacups, gather round.

Molly Gail, I heard you say

You have had a trying day.

So have I, says Hannah Lee

Wendy Ann just stares at me.

What's your story, Laura Sue?

Do you want one lump or two?

Why do you girls look so sad?

Is my special tea that bad?

Quiet now. Here comes my child

Settle down. Let's not get loud.

"Mother, what is going on?

I wondered where my dolls had gone!"

Living in the World of Fiction

It's 2057 and zombies have taken over. Buildings on the street are up in flames.

A hero is among them, his heart the only beating. This hero doesn't even have a name.

A baby when this started, this hero knows no family. He doesn't even know a mom and dad.

All he knows is chaos and the beings out to get him. Growing up with this is all he had.

Of billions of zombies, the hero has killed thousands.He knows he has a daunting task ahead.

He's always on a mission. He never gets to rest. For if he does, he'll surely end up dead.

This hero doesn't know yet, he's not the only out there, still alive and trying to survive.

Fighting off the zombies and closing in upon him, is another who was born into this life.

A woman with a heartbeat, the only other human, treks toward him with a gun strapped to her back.

When she meets the hero, they proceed to fight together, but the zombies just continue to attack.

Both of them are fine though, because this is only fiction, and none of what I said has taken place.

In the world of fiction, everything is fine, even when zombies kill the human race.

Fire and Ice

People tell me there are two different sides of me.

I don't know. I have only met one.

I'm only a child, free-spirited and wild,

Emitting more shine than the sun.

People tell me there's also a dark side,

But I just don't know what they mean.

Though many described it, I still just don't buy it.

It isn't a truth I have seen.

It scares me the horrors they've told me,

But I know there's no way that is me.

When others are down, I'm the first one around.

I'm not who they think me to be.

Abby is gone for the moment.

You'll settle for Greg, you old swine.

Abby's pathetic and way too poetic,

Just dazzling the world with her rhymes.

Yes, that was me making fun.

My words don't need to have rhythm.

I meant it that Abby's pathetic,

So deal with it. I'm not taking that back.

In fact, instead, I will add to it.

You are pathetic too.

I'm sorry, I don't know what happened.

At times, I zone out for a while.

But when I come back into focus,

I come back to greet you with smiles.

People tell me there are two different sides of me.

I don't know. I have only met one.

I'm only a child, free-spirited and wild,

Emitting more shine than the sun.

Insecurities

Distant Eyes

They're watching me. I feel their stares.

Why do they watch me? No one cares.

I try to hide but it's no use.

I feel constrained. Just let me loose!

They're watching me. I don't know why.

Do they like watching someone cry?

Nowhere to turn. I'm trapped, you see.

I wish they would just let me be.

I'll try to sleep, 'cause when I dream,

They'll watch me but won't hear me scream.

Notice Me

I walk quickly through these crowded halls, dragging my fingertips along the walls.

Hoping for just a bit of stability, hiding way deep down behind my fragility.

Looking for answers to questions unasked, wanting to reveal myself while wearing a mask.

Hoping and searching and crying and praying, ready to go but continue delaying.

I want to be seen, but without all the showing, to move this boat forward without all the rowing.

Notice me standing here stating my fears, speaking courageously for no one to hear.

Crumbling while mumbling the feelings inside of me, hopelessly venting to only my diary.

Consumed by Bullies

I know you won't believe me,

But I'm not really here

I died at half past midnight

On my birthday, just last year.

Just go and ask my mother

She's crying as we speak

My so-called friends will tell you

That you're dealing with a freak.

But let me back the train up,

Explain what it's about,

Before I lose the one friend

Who has never thrown me out.

It started back in preschool,

When I was only three

Somebody pulled my pants down,

And the kids all laughed at me.

My father taught me wrestling,

But it was just no use

Throughout my years of schooling,

I have suffered great abuse.

The bullies overwhelmed me

They made me feel so small

They drained the life inside me

'til I had no life at all.

I met someone in college

Samantha is her name

She acted like she loved me,

But she played me like a game.

And even with my family,

I felt so out of place

Just like a total stranger,

Or a man from outer space.

I really hate to tell you

Don't want to bring you down

I know you've always been there

You're my only friend in town.

One night, when you were sleeping,

I wanted this to end

Please say you will forgive me

But I had no choice, my friend.

Won't tell you how I did it

It's best if you don't know

But there's no turning back now,

And I really have to go.

We've been best friends since grade school,

When you moved in next door

I kept these feelings hidden,

When I should have told you more.

When others were disheartening,

You always were so nice

Before I go forever,

I will leave you this advice...

Don't follow in my footsteps

Be positive and free

Don't be consumed by others,

Or you'll end up just like me.

One Step Away

I'm one step away from being good enough.

I'm one step away from my dreams.

I swear I'm so close, I can taste it.

I swear I'm so far, I could scream.

I'm one step away from being brave enough.

Just one step away from taking a chance.

Each time I take half a step forward,

I step backward, as if it's a dance.

But this is the dance of life.

If I don't take that step, I won't make it.

And I know I must actually move.

It isn't as if I can fake it.

I'm one step away from being good enough.

But I feel like I'm glued to the floor.

So, I stand here in place, just staring ahead

Always wanting more.

Reflections

Staring long and hard

Into the glass upon my wall

Who is that person standing there?

I don't know her at all.

Looking even deeper

Getting lost in my own eyes

Is it me I am not fond of,

Or the world that I despise?

Lost in my emotions

I reach out to touch my hand

The reflection of my tears

Has left me frozen where I stand.

Reflections of the present

And reflections of the past

They lead me into darkness

Where my troubles seem so vast.

Reflections of my whole life

And the way things used to be

And dreams of a new life

Where I can love the girl I see.

Halloween

Halloween is the only day I've ever felt myself.

Masks and snacks and orange and black and spiders on the shelf.

The only day of 365 that not a soul critiques.

Doesn't matter black or white or short or just a geek.

Paint a face and get dressed up to write a different story.

Sometimes, it's a fantasy when life is dull or boring.

The first of May, I sit and pray the day will get here faster,

For if it's any other day, my life is just disaster.

Confusion

I'm negative, I'm positive

I'm ugly, then I'm not

The clouds, they cry; the sun, he smiles

I'm cold, and then I'm hot.

I'm facing left, I'm turning right

The path, she's straight ahead

I'm counting sheep, I'm resting deep

Awake, asleep in bed.

I'm reaching out, I'm pulling back

I scream, and then I dance

I'm giving up on everything

And then I take a chance.

I hate the world, I love you all

I hurt, I feel no pain

I'm drowning in the desert and

I'm burning in the rain.

I make no sense, I'm logical

I guess I'm just confused

Why would I sit here sulking

When I know I am amused?

I struggle, yet I've got this now

Just trying to make sense

Confusion takes on many forms,

With lack of confidence.

So maybe I'm not here, nor there

Don't see what others see

If I'm not proud of who I am,

Confusion conquers me.

Losing the Race of Life

Life is a race, and I'm losing.

I'm dragging so slowly behind.

No degree on my wall

No ring on my finger

No boyfriend or girlfriend or child.

Nothing to show I've made progress.

Still working the same 9 to 5.

No car of my own yet

No credit or loan debt

There's barely a sign I'm alive.

I don't post my milestones online.

If I did, there'd be nothing to post.

For I have done nothing

I have been nowhere

I'm feeling as if I'm a ghost.

I guess I'll just keep my routine.

'Cause really it's all that I have.

Keep dragging my feet

Keep walking in place

'Cause really it isn't that bad.

Rumors

Believed and spread like wildfire, but never really true.

Guaranteed to ruin reputations.

Rumors come and go, but they come back around anew.

And this is what has caused my contemplations.

I contemplate my worth.

I contemplate my life.

I contemplate just leaving, starting fresh.

Too many have spread lies.

I'm starting to believe them.

Now I as well have something to detest.

I detest the rumors and all they have destroyed.

I detest the person they created.

But when the day is over, what I detest the most:

I began the rumors out of hatred.

Youngest of Seven

Lia got to play soccer

Paul got to be in band

Monica played violin

Trish got to visit Japan.

Josh got to play piano

Nya played guitar

I sit at home, bored and alone,

While they focus on their art.

Four of them are grown now

Their life is fun and wild

The other two are always out,

Leaving me an only child.

Bonded to six siblings

You'd think I'd have a friend

But all I have are books and music

That I of course got secondhand.

The youngest one of seven

I get mixed in with the crowd

But my siblings are so talented

I'm told to just be proud.

It's time to start my own journey

So, I jump ship and leave a note

I have a million passions

There's no telling where I'll go.

164

It's time to start my own journey

So, I jump ship and leave a note

I have a million passions

There's no telling where I'll go.

Neglected

I always feel neglected

Like I'm a speck of dust,

Like others are the shiny chrome

And I'm the spot of rust.

I am the one at parties

Who always hides away

While other people chat a lot

I've got no words to say.

When you speak, people listen

When I speak, I'm ignored

When they're with you, they have a blast

When they're with me, they're bored.

I cannot say I blame them

I often bore myself

It's like the whole world rides the sleigh

And I sit on the shelf.

I'd like someone to talk to

Who cares to hear my voice

But sadly, that will never be

I have no other choice.

Perhaps my words unspoken

Will be heard when I'm gone

I'll never know neglect again

My soul will carry on.

166 ALISON BRETT AND TINA MICHELLE

Perhaps my words unspoken

Will be heard when I'm gone

I'll never know neglect again

My soul will carry on.

Jealousy

She's beautiful as fallen snow upon the forest trees.

Some people tell me I am pretty, only to appease.

Her intellect is unsurpassed; there's nothing she can't do.

I told her many times before, "I wish I were like you."

When we go out, all eyes on her, and I am like a ghost.

And yet, she's vastly modest, and she never tends to boast.

So, why do I feel anger, like I want to take her down?

She's supposed to be my best friend, but I don't want her around.

I try to keep my thoughts at bay, so I don't harm my friend,

But jealousy is evil, and the victor in the end.

My Stutter

I sit at the table for Thanksgiving dinner

I ask him to pass me the bu bu bu butter

There they go laughing unkindly again

They don't understand what it feels like to stutter.

I don't know why I kee kee keep attending

I thought holidays were supposed to be special

But I am the jester, amusing the crowd

They are Lake Superior; I'm just the vessel.

I am a good person like all who surround me

But I'm always getting unwanted attention

If they ta ta talked like me all of the time,

I wouldn't be subject to their condescension.

I think I'll just sit here and feast on the turkey

I won't say a word; I'll just listen to others

They want entertainment; I will not oblige

They'll have to converse with ma my boring brothers.

Well, time to go now to my place of non-judgement

My blanket awaits, and my pillows are calling

I'm thinking that next year, I'll just stay at home

This group could not be any le less enthralling.

I know I'll be missed; they'll be lacking amusement

But there is a lesson that needs to be taken

If they think I'll sit and endure disrespect,

I'm afraid that they're all ve ve very mistaken.

Fatigued

Images of twigs and branches

Adding beauty to the tree

Haven't eaten food for days now

Water will suffice for me.

I am heavy as the wind blows

Ninety pounds and five foot three

Weighted down like Birch and Redwood

Feeling like I am the tree.

I should wait until tomorrow

Don't need food; I'll be okay

Plants and trees can grow on water

I can make it one more day.

I am feeling quite fatigued now

Lying down like fallen leaves

Why have I become so sleepy?

I'll just lie here in the breeze.

I will sleep until tomorrow

When I wake, I'll be alright

Bring me water in the morning

Eyes are heavy now; goodnight.

Three Sizes Down from Four

Looking in the mirror, I don't like what I see.

I see a girl who's lacking with abundance.

Too much extra meat on bones that almost touch the surface.

I'm broken, and yet, desperately I want this.

It feels it was just yesterday, I dropped down to size three.

Now, here I am, three sizes down from four.

I know I should be satisfied, but it'll never be enough.

I find that I just keep on wanting more.

I want a slimmer size, but just one more is out there.

I'm not sure where I'll go when I achieve it.

I want to say that zero will finally be enough.

But I guess I'm just not sure if I believe it.

I know this makes no sense, but the mirror doesn't lie.

And though pounds are gone, the weight still seems to follow.

Three sizes down from four, and just one more to go.

I feel full beside a reflection that is hollow.

Hopelessness, Trauma, and Obsessions

Faith

There's a higher power, I know it.

So, why will he not show it?

Why does he insist I walk my own path? I might blow it.

Why does he repeat to me, "You'll reap it, if you sow it."

I don't know all the answers, but there's a higher power, I know it.

I walk the road less traveled, with hopes to see him along the way.

I don't see him. I can't see far at all, so come what may.

I don't know what would come for me if I should choose to stay.

So, I continue moving, and while I do, I pray.

I walk the road less traveled, with hopes to see him along the way.

There's something here. I feel it.

I just need to reveal it.

Layer after layer, it is hidden, but I peel it.

If my fate is just not quite yet written, then I'll seal it.

If my life is not my own to have, then I will steal it.

There's a higher power, I knew it.

I know because I got through it.

I guess I don't need proof anymore. I guess that I outgrew it.

I learned that life is easier if you just get up and do it.

But I was never on my own. The lord was there, I knew it.

Physical Dilemma

I am having trouble breathing today.

There is a heaviness in my chest.

I am having trouble sleeping today.

And laying my thoughts to rest.

I think I feel a loss in circulation to my arms.

I think I have a cough.

I am feeling quite alarmed.

Something must be wrong. Just living seems a challenge.

Yesterday was fine. Today, I am off balance.

I can't go to the doctor. I know what they would say.

We ran every test we could. The results say you're okay.

Veered Off Course

I have something to tell you! I've been waiting all day.

Goodness, where do I start? There's just so much to say!

I saw the prettiest bird with the coolest of colors,

And it reminded me of last year when we were under the covers,

Trying to determine what color we would paint the room,

But it ended up black because we decided too soon.

I miss those days! They remind me of Autumn,

When we got our first dog, but someone else almost bought him,

But then he was ours, and he loved us so much,

But now I'm just thinking how he got hit by that truck.

Huh. Anyway, I think that's all I had to say.

Let's talk about something else, I guess. How was your day?

You know what? Everything you say is just irritating right now,

And you're disturbing the neighbors. You're being too loud!

You're disturbing me too. Just leave! Go! Get out!

I didn't mean that. Please stay. I think I'd better lie down.

I Still

I still hear the gunshots daily at nine

I still won't watch the news

I still won't travel

I still wake up crying and often get the blues

I still have Bentley, my dog with a vest

I still feel quite paranoid that maybe I'm next

I still am in pain

I still get the shakes

I still wake at 4 just to scream out your name

I still run for cover

I still have my guard up

I still won't let people see me

I still won't tell others my story

I still don't think they would relieve me.

Insomnia

I find it hard to function; I don't get the sleep I need

I'm searching for solutions that will help me to succeed.

I lie awake in bed all night, not knowing what to do

Relaxing is so hard for me, but that is nothing new.

My mind is like a racing car, forever on the track

And once those wheels start spinning fast, there is no turning back.

I've tried the medications that the doctors recommend

They always give me headaches and do nothing in the end.

And then you hear the old cliché, I should be counting sheep

But that is so nonsensical and will not help me sleep.

My boss says I am in a fog and others would agree

I'm like a branch that's slowly disconnecting from the tree.

Because of this, my future's dim; I don't know what's in store

I'll just lie here in bed again and try to sleep once more.

Lethal Germs

Help me; I'm surrounded by a multitude of grime

I'm headed to the sink to wash my hands a seventh time.

Bacteria inhabits my world at every turn

And hanging with a crowd this large is reason for concern.

I have a thumb print on my glass; I know it isn't mine

So, now I'll need to get myself another glass of wine.

I cannot eat the food, as I am not sure where it's been

I feel like there are maggots crawling underneath my skin.

Can we get out of here right now? I really must get home

I need to clean my room again and hide out there alone.

Obsessed

I sit outside your house each night,

just staring at your door

And then I drive back home unsure

of what I'm searching for.

I hop on social media

more often than I should

I have no time for other things

and that cannot be good.

I'm on your page an awful lot,

like fifty times a day

I want to see into your world,

for mine is dim and gray.

I should just call and say hello,

but I am much too shy

I'm pretty sure with your finesse,

I'm not your type of guy.

If I were to get close to you,

I would feel out of place

So, I'll just watch from far away

and hope to see your face.

I guess you know about me now

At last, I have confessed

I'm living my dreams through your eyes

It looks like I'm obsessed.

Fear

Shadows in the Dark

Leave the door open

Well, just a crack

The nightmares may keep me awake

Fuming, and looming, and all but consuming me,

Telling me life is at stake.

Keep the TV on

Volume on low

The voices soothe and amuse me.

They cancel the sound of the noises I hear,

The noises that taunt and abuse me.

Leave the light on

Just a bit,

So that I can see my way.

I need these comforts every night

To get me through the day.

The Unknown

Fearful of the present.

Terrified of the past.

Tortured by the future,

even though it happens last.

Scared of the not knowing.

Wondering what will become.

Never really getting there.

Always feeling numb.

Thoughts too far from words.

Words too far from truth.

Quickly young to old.

Always losing youth.

Flying from the nest.

Wondering where I've flown.

Can't stop me from fearing

All parts of the unknown.

Cold Feet

I'm dressed in satin and white lace. My mother's combing my hair.

She asks me which necklace I think I'll wear. I tell her I don't care.

"This one," I guess. I put it on, trying not to cause a stir.

She looks at me in the mirror, but I don't look back at her.

She asks me if I'm okay and tells me I'm looking rather flushed.

I tell her I need a minute. I think I might throw up.

I storm out of that room so fast, that I nearly trip and fall.

The faces are all a blur, as I race the wrong way down the hall.

The best man tries to stop me and asks me where I'm going.

My mother-in-law drops her jaw and tells me I'm positively glowing.

I quickly hurry past them and run across the lawn.

I barely even notice when the sprinklers come on.

My heels are sinking into mud, and my dress is soaking wet.

People are walking toward me, and I'm trying not to fret.

I've all but destroyed this day when my fiancé's eyes meet mine.

I hug him and tell him my feet are cold, but otherwise, I'm fine.

Standing at the altar, those fears all dissipate.

I say, "I do," and kiss his lips, and I swear, it feels like fate.

Disturbing Dreams

Heart beating fast, all through the night

Being chased, running fast, feeling great fright.

Who are these men, seeking to kill?

Grabbing me, hurting me, while I stand still.

Frozen I stand, trying to scream

Not a sound, it's no use, I'm in a dream.

When I'm awake, I am still tense

Panicky, timorous, nothing makes sense.

I'm so afraid, to go to bed

Scary dreams, endless thoughts, mess with my head.

Can't fight the sleep, my eyes are closed

Here I go, back to dreams, fully exposed.

I See Ghosts

I saw him standing by my bed

My eyes were open wide

But suddenly he disappeared

And I was petrified.

His presence inexplicable

He died one year ago

He whispered some specific things

That only I would know.

The next day, I saw Adeline

And she's not even here

She moved to Frankfurt Germany

December of last year.

She told me that my mom's alive

Her voice was like a song

But when I checked my mother's grave

I knew that she was wrong.

And Michael comes here every day

And shares his deep desires

He said that he's the only one

Survivor of the fires.

Sweet Peggy Jane, she's only five

I know she needs a friend

She said she lived in foster homes

Until her bitter end.

I wonder who will visit me

Today and days ahead

They're all I have for company

Until I, too, am dead.

Perserverance

Perspective

Without dark, there'd be no light.

Without pain, there'd be no pleasure.

Without sadness, there'd be no happiness.

Without failure, we wouldn't feel success.

Without constraints, we wouldn't feel freedom.

Without heartbreak, we wouldn't feel love.

We recognize the greatest feelings by the opposites that plague us.

We recognize the upsides by the downsides that they lack.

Be mindful, if you wish the bad away.

Another may just wish to have it back.

Say it Silently

Say it silently, but with the power of one thousand words.

Say it silently, because when you say it aloud, it always hurts.

Say it silently, because when it is heard, it makes it all too real.

Say it silently, because the emotions are yours, to hold and to feel.

Say it silently, because no one else should be empowered to tear you down.

Say it silently. Say it for you. Say it with meaning. Say it and stand your ground.

The first step is the hardest, but the steps are yours to climb. So, go on and say it silently.

Be empowered and speak your mind.